D0230392

October, 1926. Sir Alan Cobham flying low over Westminster Bridge after his record flight from Australia.

Between the Wars
BRITAIN
in Photographs

Introduction and commentaries by
JULIAN SYMONS

B. T. Batsford Ltd
London

© Julian Symons 1972

First published 1972
Second impression 1985

All rights reserved. No part of this publication may be
reproduced in any form or by any means without permission
from the publishers

ISBN 0 7134 0121 4

Printed and bound in Great Britain by
Anchor Brendon Ltd, Tiptree, Essex
for the publishers
B. T. Batsford Ltd
4 Fitzhardinge Street
London W1H 0AH

CONTENTS

ACKNOWLEDGEMENTS

The Author and Publisher would like to thank the following for permission to reproduce photographs: Architectural Review (26); Fox Photos Ltd (181, 185, 187, 188); Glasgow Herald & Evening Times (122); John Vickers (154); National Film Archive (159); Radio Times Hulton Picture Library (2, 4, 10–14, 23, 31, 32, 34, 37, 38, 40–44, 46, 47, 50, 52, 53, 55, 56, 60–62, 71, 76, 77, 84, 86–88, 90, 91, 94, 95, 98, 99, 101, 102, 120, 124, 125, 127, 129, 130, 136, 137, 140, 143, 147, 150–153, 155, 158, 160, 162–164, 167–170, 178–180, 182, 184, 186); Topix (7, 9).

INTRODUCTION

Every picture tells a story, and every story may be true, but the truth it tells is partial and single, not general and total. When we read a book of memoirs we recognise that it is only one man's evidence of what took place, and we check it by documents and by what other people wrote and said. Looking at a picture does not prompt this immediate doubt, and because we tend to accept what we see, pictures offer the kind of truth through which it is easy to tell lies. A picture of two policemen frog-marching a striker can often be matched by a picture of two strikers attacking a policeman. Which picture do you look at, or if you are making this kind of book, which do you use? If you use both, do they cancel each other out? Not at all. They simply confirm the views already held by the people who look at the pictures, about the relative merits of policemen versus strikers.

What follows, then, is personal: a personal portrait of Britain between the Wars seen through the eyes of a non-party Leftist, committed enough, however, to have no doubt about which side he is on when he sees a worker in conflict with his natural enemy (in George Orwell's phrase) a policeman. It would be easy to make a dozen different portraits of those two strange decades. They could be shown as an idyllic time when prices were lower, beaches cleaner, roads less crowded, and when almost any middle-class family had a servant who lived in. For some people the most emphatic truths about these years are that in them great stretches of beautiful British countryside were open to the traveller and yet remained unspoiled, and that the interests of country people had not been made identical with those of townspeople by television. They can be seen as years of amateurism in sport, comparative innocence in sex, and of respect for tradition.

These portraits would not be wholly untrue, yet none of them would convey the way things looked at the time. The distinguishing feature of the period was the enormous changes in almost every aspect of life, changes foreseen by few people when the fighting stopped. The drinkers and dancers at the Ritz and in the East End shown among the early pictures were celebrating not only the end of the War, but also a return to the settled society of the pre-war world. Many people fought the War to preserve the past, and anybody who was more

3   (overleaf) 'Escaping humming down arterial roads' moved cars and motor cycles. Wrotham Hill Kent, in the Thirties.

than 40 years old in 1914 was almost certain to dislike the present into which he was forcibly ushered. The struggle between past and present, between the hand plough and the motor tractor, the craftsman and the factory, is what most clearly gives character to British life in the Twenties and Thirties. The new world was above all one in which people moved about faster. Before August, 1914, the motor car was a rich man's toy. After 1919 it moved more quickly, broke down less frequently, and eventually was produced in great numbers. Yet car ownership still remained a badge of class and income. Manual workers, city clerks and dustmen did not own cars. They were no longer a privilege or amusement of the rich, but car ownership was the fulfilment of a social aspiration, a mark that you were a little better than your neighbours.

Many middle-aged and middle-class people felt that life as a whole was becoming more mechanical. You might use your motor car to go to a cinema, there to watch a machine-made show which with the coming of sound became very distinctively American. Both motor car and cinema were habit-forming pieces of machinery, and the cinema involved only watching, not participation. There was strong deprecation of the way in which people flocked to what we now call spectator sports, like dog racing and dirt-track racing. Mass production of almost everything in factories was said to be wiping out individual skills. And as the years passed, art too was less and less made in a middle-class image.

For such people one solace remained. Among so many changes, class barriers remained reassuringly firm. Britain between the Wars was a deeply class-conscious society, with forms of social conduct, habits of speech, styles of dress, so different between one class and another that for all except the most adept or skilfully imitative they made an unbridgeable chasm. Yet the levelling pressures exerted by motoring and the cinema did prompt changes even here, which seemed important then although they may now look trivial. An instance from sport may stand for much else. In 1922 *The Times* moved cautiously in the direction of democracy by dropping the prefix 'Mr' before the names of amateur cricketers, although they retained initials while professionals were designated only by a surname, so that the score cards of Gentlemen *v* Players matches look now distinctly odd. Another concession was made when amateurs and professionals came out of the same entrance. Resistance to the idea of a professional captain, however, remained strong. Yorkshire, who lacked good amateurs, had a captain at one time who batted generally at Number 11, did not bowl, and was an indifferent field. He was, however, an amateur.

These were the visible shapes of life, but over much of the period there hung, for young and old alike, a cloudy disturbed sense that they lived in a society at odds with itself. The social injustice of the period was extreme, and although the disparities of wealth and poverty were kept from many by the fact that they had never met a miner or a factory worker (as many people today have never met a militant trade unionist), there was still an uneasy feeling among people who lived comfortably that something drastic or dramatic should be done to help the unemployed. With this went a consciousness that the great domestic events of the time, the Wembley Exhibition, the General Strike, the Abdication, were in some sense shams, the first an unsuccessful attempt to assert a fading Empire's solidarity and supremacy, the second a feeble and unintended gesture towards revolution, the third a game of musical chairs that changed nothing of importance. It was the timid ineptness of successive Governments and of working-class movements alike, that drove many to look for solutions in Communism and Fascism.

In retrospect the whole period looks like an interregnum between the savage realities of two wars, but again of course it was not like that for those who lived through it. The pictures as one turns them over are optimistic, sad, nostalgic, unbelievable. Were there actually Bright Young Things, did people really wear Oxford bags? Is it possible to look without indignation, even now, at the Jarrow Marchers? When one thinks of the resources Britain possessed at this time, and then of the refusal or inability to use them to achieve any measure of social equality, one can only marvel at the timidity and imperceptiveness of the politicians who held power.

Julian Symons

BRITAIN'S CHANGING FACE

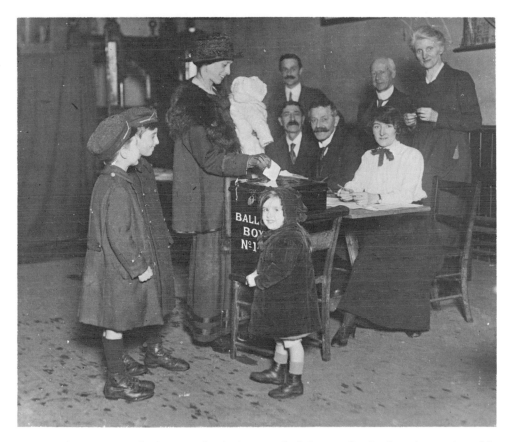

4 December, 1918. At the 'coupon election' women had the vote for the first time, and used it extensively. The result was an overwhelming victory for the Lloyd George coalition. The Asquithian Liberals lost nearly 100 seats, including Asquith's own. Labour polled heavily, and gained 20 seats. For the Liberals it was the end of power, for Labour the first glimpse of it.

5 The Armistice on 11 November 1918, was greeted with wild enthusiasm. Cheering crowds in London streets and outside Buckingham Palace were only a small part of it. In many towns and cities all business was suspended. Big Ben, which had been silent, struck the hours again. Fortunes were made by selling small flags in the streets. There were dozens of celebrations like this one at the Ritz Hotel.

6   Armistice celebrations in London's East End. All the streets in slum districts were vivid with flags. 'The Cinderella of the great household which is London' was 'transformed from drabness to a place of blazing colour', as one paper put it.

7 WAACS being demobilised at Bostall Heath, September, 1919. The general expectation was that, once women were out of uniform and out of factories, they would revert to their status of household helps and bedmates. But this was not what happened. The new women were part of the new world.

8 (*left*) An Oxford college dining room, probably in the Thirties.

9 (*below*) Girton held its Jubilee celebrations on 26 July 1919. H. A. L. Fisher in his address congratulated the College on disturbing 'nothing that was venerable or good in the ancient discipline of the University', and certainly to all appearance the celebration might have been held in 1900.

10 The police strike of August, 1919, was the result of the authorities' determined resistance to the idea of a Police Union. The picture shows men of London's 'B' Division at the beginning of the strike. It was a complete failure. Only a few hundred men came out in London, although in Liverpool more than half the police force were on strike, and there was considerable support also in Birmingham. After the strike collapsed, all the men involved were dismissed from the force without pension, or any compensation for past service. As late as 1945, a deputation from the Association of Police Strikers pleaded with the Labour Prime Minister, Clement Attlee, for a small pension to be given to those strikers still alive. 26 years earlier Attlee, then Mayor of Stepney, had supported their cause. Now they got a stony answer.

11 and 12 The Thirties did not have a monopoly of demonstrations. This march by the largely feminine No More War League took place in July, 1923. Anti-war marches were a regular feature of the British scene between the wars.

13 On the night of 30 November 1936, almost the whole of the Crystal Palace was destroyed. The fire, which raged unstoppably, burned the building in three hours. The glow was seen at Brighton, and throughout most of London it looked like an exaggerated orange sunset.

So died a remarkable building of glass and iron which, when projected by Sir Joseph Paxton in the 1850s, was jeered at as a structure that would not survive the first storm. Transported from Hyde Park to Sydenham, and there increased in length to the distance of almost half a mile, it was popular for the holding of fêtes, plays, Saturday concerts. In the twentieth century it fell on unprofitable times, and in 1911 sale by auction was threatened, although not carried out. In its last years this great glass elephant was held in much affection by Londoners. At the time of its destruction a show of waxworks was on display.

14 A salvage man with some of the waxworks at Madame Tussaud's, which was temporarily closed in March, 1925, as the result of a fire.

15 The annual Michaelmas Fair, like this one at Brent in Devon, continued between the Wars, organised and attended by very much the same sort of people.

17 (*overleaf*) A continuing tradition is suggested in this tranquil picture of Piccadilly. The horse and carriage is an advertising device.

16   A fine aerial view of London's Caledonian Market.

18 Ceremonies and rituals emphasise the continuing power of tradition. Dancing round the maypole at Shipton on Stour, Warwickshire.

19 *Drunk with steam-organs, thigh-rub and cream soda.*
Louis MacNeice

20 (*top*) Felix the Cat for the Twenties, Mickey Mouse for the Thirties. No child's bedroom before World War I looked remotely like this.

21 (*bottom*) A modern kitchen in the Thirties with lots of electric gadgets, including the clock.

22 (*top*) Decorations for Clive Bell's library, done by Duncan Grant and Vanessa Bell. The fussy extravagance (consider the purely ornamental fireplace) is typical of one British style, but there were others. Period, mid-Twenties.

23 (*bottom*) This 'smoking suit' for women, *circa* 1922, has its period charm. So does the smoker.

24 and 25 Two typical examples of inter-war housing. The bow-fronted houses are at Camberley in Surrey, but they could have been duplicated in almost any large town or suburb.

26 and 27 Two houses of the Thirties, at Bognor Regis (*above*) and Chelsea. Clean, bare and assured, deliberately avoiding ornament, they are typical advanced architecture of the period.

28 The De La Warr Pavilion, Bexhill (*above*), a building influenced by European models. (*opposite top*) The *Daily Express* building in Fleet Street (1934) is a misapplication of Bauhaus ideas, but remains impressive in its thrusting vulgarity.

29 (*opposite below*) A prison-like block of flats (London, 1934). The unhappy thing about slum clearance, then as now, is that it pays little attention to the emotional needs of slum-dwellers.

31 and 32   There was little new school and University building, and most of what was done lacked imagination. The new building at Caterham School (*below*) was opened by the Bishop of Birmingham. Erith Middle Park School (*right*) was designed to form a sun trap, with direct access from all infants' classes to their playground, and a southerly aspect for every classroom. It is unfortunate that the girls are moving in a circle strongly reminiscent of a prison walk.

33 (*left*) Children in school. The picture gives an idea of the large classes and frequently depressing conditions.

34 Woolworths did not change much, although the top price was no longer sixpence.

35 Among the traditions that stayed untouched was that of Harrods, which differed from Harrods past and future only in the style of its window display.

36 More tradition: high tea, with cold ham, and eggs, kippers or haddock.

GETTING ABOUT FASTER

37 The recommended 'spring jazz costume' for girl motor cyclists in 1925.

38 (*overleaf*) A traffic jam at the Bank of England, 1922. Horse-drawn traffic, like the horse and cart here sandwiched between buses, already looks anachronistic.

39 and 40   The omnipresent tramcar, in Oxford Street, Manchester (*left*), and (*below*) at the Elephant and Castle in South London. The pictures suggest how difficult tramcars made things for other traffic.

41, 42 and 43 Motoring for pleasure. (*below*) Tooting High Street on Derby Day, 1922. (*opposite*) two pictures of cars and buses arriving at Ascot, 1920.

44 The idea of controlling traffic mechanically came in the Twenties. The first traffic lights (*below*) were installed in 1926, with control boxes like this one at the top of St James's Street in London. The policeman is there, presumably, to make sure that the signals are obeyed.

45 (*opposite*) Belisha beacons, at which 'a motorist must either slow down or stop to allow pedestrians to cross the street', were first seen in 1934 at the instance of Leslie Hore-Belisha, who thus achieved a small immortality.

46   At the 1922 Olympia and White City Motor Show the cheapest cars like the Rover, GN and Jowett, cost from £180 to £225. The four cylinder Austin 7 also cost £225, while what was called the 'family car', like the Cubitt, Dodge, Overland, Ruston-Hornsby and Armstrong Siddeley, went up to £600.

   The picture shows the most unusual car of the 1922 show, the solid-tyre Trojan. This was a 2-stroke, which kept its engine under the floorboards, and was driven by epicyclic gearing with a final duplex chain. The tyres, which were guaranteed for 15,000 miles, were used with a special cantilever suspension. The price was around £200.

47 Part of the Motor Show in the late Twenties, when cars were becoming both more powerful and cheaper.

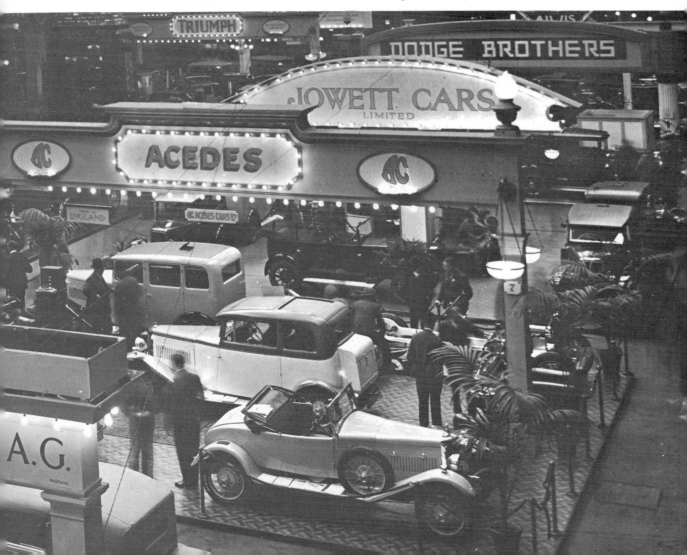

48 (*above*) Waterloo Station, August 1933. Waiting for a holiday train. The railways lost money, there were (as there still are) complaints about their bad time-keeping and service, but they retained their supremacy as a means of holiday travel.

49 (*left*) The impressive interior of Cockfosters Underground station (1934)

50 (*right*) Ticket machines at the new Piccadilly Circus station (1928).

51 (*above*) The first transatlantic flight. Captain John Alcock and Lieutenant Arthur Whitten Brown leave New-foundland in their Vickers Vimy bomber, 14 June, 1919. Their total flying time was 16 hours 12 minutes. Both were knighted.

52 (*left*) The first mail flown from Australia to Britain arrives at Croydon, in May, 1931.

53 (*above*) Jim and Amy Mollison, breakers of flying records, beside their de Havilland Puss Moth *The Heart's Content*, February, 1933.

54 (*below*) The passenger plane 'Golden Clipper' leaving Croydon for Paris in 1933. The plane crossed in the record time of 92 minutes.

55 The R.101 at the mooring mast in Cardington. On its promenade deck were chairs and a rail, there was a lounge 60 feet long, and a handsome dining saloon. Many people believed that the future of passenger air travel lay with the airship, not the aeroplane.

In October, 1930, the R.101 crashed in France on a test flight. Lord Thomson, the Air Minister, and Sir Sefton Brancker, Director of Civil Aviation, were among the 50-odd passengers. With the crash (there were only six survivors) British belief in the airship died for ever.

56 Two bridesmaids at a society wedding.

57 (*overleaf*) Ascot, 1938, the Royal Hunt Cup. For the moment, total concentration on the race.

58 (*opposite*) The biggest society wedding crowd in living memory attended the wedding of the American amateur golfer Charles Sweeney and Margaret Whigham at Brompton Oratory.

59 and 60 (*above and below*) Henley Regatta, a joint rowing and social occasion. Those who knew Henley before World War I deplored some of the innovations. The course was changed, there were too many foreign entries, Oxford rowing was eclipsed, and they were actually using gramophones on some of the boats.

61   (*above*) A group of debutantes at Queen Charlotte's Birthday Ball, May 1931.

62   (*left*) 'Bright Young Things' (a newspaper label which stuck) in a snowball fight at a roof-garden party.

63   Guests at the Dorchester watching the show put on by the Midnight Follies girls from New York, 1933.

64   At any British upper class social occasion the importance of being seen is supreme. Here are the Highland Games at Aboyne, with a selection of peers and their wives on display.

65 *Ere Jorrocks was and yet to be*
The Honourable Crasher,
There used to hunt from Nineveh
A customer called Ashur

wrote the author of a history of fox-hunting, in defence of the sport which Oscar Wilde summed up as 'the unspeakable in pursuit of the uneatable'. Certainly few eat the fox, but are his hunters unspeakable? Most at this time had private incomes, not many were intellectuals, but the judgement seems harsh. With its rituals, and its particularities of dress, hunting emphasises how closely such a class pleasure is associated with the need to dress up and to be seen on display.

THE PEOPLE'S PLEASURES

66 *Windsor Lad* winning the St. Leger, 1934.

67 Greyhound racing at Clapton Stadium, 1933. The sport, introduced to Britain in 1926, was immediately successful. It provided an easy alternative to horse racing as a means of gambling.

68 The feeling of being one among several thousand people supporting a common cause is part of the pleasure in watching a football match. The inter-war years drew bigger crowds than the more glamorous stars of today can attract. Chelsea versus Wolverhampton Wanderers, Stamford Bridge, 1933 (*above*).

69 (*opposite*) Sir Frederick Wall, the 75-year-old President of the Football Association, gives the ball a kick at Wembley before making Cup Final preparations.

70 and 71 Brighton beach (*left*). A daring bathing costume (the phrase of the period) of 1921 (*below*).

72 Blackpool beach in August, 1933, seen from the Tower. The upper class on holiday, and today the middle class too, search for solitude. The working class look for other people. The typical working-class holiday between the wars was one week or two at a boarding house in a seaside resort during its most crowded weeks. The men drank, the women sat on the beach, the children paddled, bathed, dug. The pattern is still discernible in a different form at Butlin's or Pontin's.

73 The idea of hiking – discovering the country on foot – started in the middle Twenties, and became steadily more popular. Generally hikers took a train out of their town or city before starting to walk.

74 The pub, one of the people's primary pleasures. This is the village pub at Bradford Abbas, Dorset, complete with the still extant game of bar skittles.

75 The Glen Cinema, Glasgow, in the Twenties. W. H. Auden imagined the working class sitting 'in the fug Of talkie houses for a drug', and the cinema was the biggest drug, or the most soothing amusement, of the time. Hollywood grew, stars were manufactured, the cinemagoer was conditioned to an American version of unreality.

76 and 77 If cinemas were Dream Palaces, should they not look like them? At the Granada, Tooting (1931), the hall and mirrors (*below*) were designed by glass experts, the interior (*right*) looks like a secular church.

78 Kate Carney

79 Nellie Wallace

80 George Formby

81 Sir Harry Lauder

82 Billy Bennett

84 George Robey

83 Harry Tate

85 Will Fyffe.

Connoisseurs of the music hall agree that by the end of World War I it had been mortally wounded by the cinema, and that the musical revue of the Twenties killed it off. For those who grew up in the Twenties, though, it seemed that music hall stars still existed, and even flourished. Some had made their reputations earlier, but all were extremely popular in the inter-war years.

86–88 The Wembley Exhibition was the most remarkable public show of these two decades. King George V opening the Exhibition, April, 1924 (*opposite*). Part of the Indian building (*right*). The Nigerian village (*below*) nearing completion. It proved a great favourite.

NIGERIA
AREA. 345,000 SQUARE MILES
POPULATION. 18,700,000

THE SPORTS THEY WATCHED

89 (*opposite*) A view of the crowd at the first Test at Trent Bridge, 1934 (*below*).

90 (*above*) The Oval Test match, 1926, and England's first victory against Australia in a Test series since the War. Woolley catching the Australian captain Collins in the slips.

91 (*above*) Suzanne Lenglen at Wimbledon in 1924. After the War women's tennis became faster and more powerful, and was no longer played almost entirely from the baseline. Lenglen dominated the scene at Wimbledon in the early Twenties. In her last year there, 1925, she lost only five games in the whole tournament.

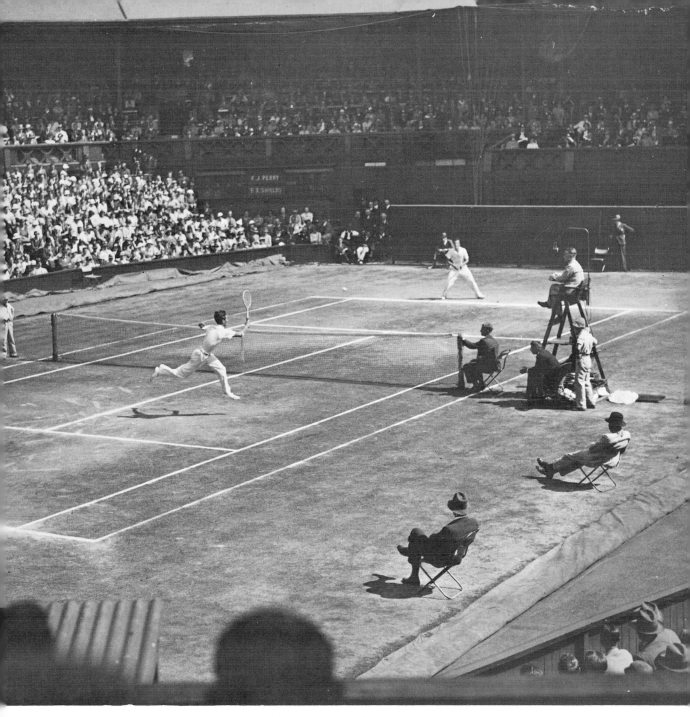

93 (*above*) Fred Perry, by far the most successful British tennis player of the last fifty years (far end) beating the American Frank Shields to retain the Davis Cup for Britain in 1934 (*above*).

92 (*opposite*) The British team: Lee, Perry, 'Bunny' Austin, G. P. Hughes.

94 (*left*) Brooklands, the great British car racing track of the inter-war years, 1930.

95 (*below*) Speedway racing, an immensely successful spectacle. 80,000 people went to Wembley to see one championship.

96 (*above*) The first Cup Final at Wembley, 1923. Bolton Wanderers (in white) beat West Ham United by two goals to nil.

97 (*right*) Dixie Dean with the F.A. Cup after Everton's defeat of Manchester City in the 1933 Cup Final. Dean broke all goal scoring records. In 1927 he scored 60 goals in 39 League matches, and 22 in other games. His final tally was 379 goals.

98 (*above*) Henry Cotton, the most famous British golfer of the time.

99 (*right*) The popularity of billiards declined steadily in the Thirties, and in many halls snooker was played almost exclusively. As a public spectacle the game was threatened by the players' skill in perfecting and then repeating a particular stroke like the nursery cannon or the losing hazard. The Australian Walter Lindrum and Tom Newman are stringing for break at Thurston's, in 1932. On this tour Lindrum made the break of 4,137 which stands as a world record.

100 (*above*) In the early Thirties the English Kaye Don and the American Gar Wood set up and broke new motorboat racing records every year. The picture shows Kaye Don giving *Miss England III* a trial run on Loch Lomond. He regained the record with a speed of 117·43 mph with this boat, but a few months later Gar Wood won it back by doing 124·86 mph with *Miss America*.

101 (*left*) Gertrude Ederle, an 18-year-old American girl, became in 1926 the first woman to swim the Channel. She took 14½ hours.

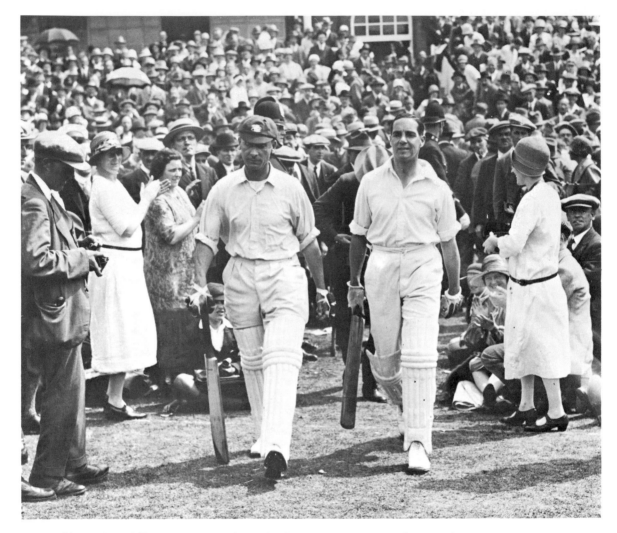

102   Hobbes and Sutcliffe go out to open the England innings against Australia at Leeds in 1926.

PEOPLE AT WORK

103   'You get into the cage, which is a steel box about as wide as a telephone box and two or three times as long. It holds ten men, but they pack like pilchards in a tin. The steel door shuts upon you, and somebody working the winding gear above drops you into the void.' George Orwell.

104 (*above*) The overseer's cabin down the pit, South Hetton Colliery, Sunderland.

105 (*right*) At the coal face. 'By no conceivable amount of effort or training could I become a coal-miner; the work would kill me in a few weeks'. George Orwell.

106 (*right*) A ploughing picture of sentimental charm.

107 (*below*) A smithy at Pyecombe, Sussex, where the crooks for South Down shepherds were made.

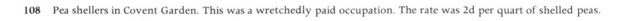

108 Pea shellers in Covent Garden. This was a wretchedly paid occupation. The rate was 2d per quart of shelled peas.

109   Hocing sugar beet by hand – again, women's work, too poorly paid for men.

110 Covent Garden. The porters were and are fiercely independent, with their own customs, habits of work, and even slang.

111 Gipsy hop pickers. 'The best pickers in our gang were a family of gipsies, five adults and a child, all of whom, of course, had picked hops every year since they could walk. In a little under three weeks these people earned exactly £10 between them.' George Orwell.

112 (*above*) manufacturing rubber clothing at Charles Mackintosh, Cambridge.

113 (*left*) Women workers (with male foreman) at the Lotus boot and shoe factory, Sheffield.

114 Women workers in the Lancashire cotton mills.

115 Resumption of work on the Cunarder 534 at John Brown's yard after a lay off. An aerial view of the deck.

116 Jubilation at the restarting of work. It is a lasting illusion among those who live in the country that Britain's prosperity is founded on its agriculture. It is, on the contrary, highly industrialised, and mass unemployment in big cities means a worsening of living conditions everywhere.

117 (*above*) A sale at Christie's in 1931. The occasion was the auction of the Bavarian Crown Jewels. The exhibit is the Wittelsbach Blue Diamond.

118 A confraternity of bowlers. Kerbstone activity outside the Stock Exchange.

119 Stockbrokers, dealers and clerks carrying on business in Throgmorton Street after the closure of the Stock Exchange at 4 p.m. on a frantic day in 1929, when fortunes were made as prices jumped.

PEOPLE NOT AT WORK

120 (*above*) Unemployed men queuing outside a Labour Exchange. During the Thirties the number of unemployed never fell far below 3 million.

121 (*opposite*) Unemployed miners at Pontypridd, who cleared a hillside of rock and sandstone, made allotments and grew vegetables.

122 (*overleaf*) The Red Flag raised at a demonstration of strikers and unemployed in Glasgow, January, 1919.

The General Strike, which lasted from 3 May to 12 May 1926, was one of the climactic events of the period. When it ended in defeat for the unions, the miners fought on alone for months, until hunger often approaching starvation forced the men back to work.

123 (*opposite, left*) Government preparations. Buses were kept ready at Westminster to take police and specials to any given spot.

124 (*opposite, below*) Some of the 'specials'. The strikers disliked them much more than they disliked the police.

125 (*below*) One of the armoured cars used in the strike.

The Times

No. 44263. London Wednesday May 5. 1926 Price 2d.

WEATHER FORECAST. Wind N.E.; fair to dull; risk of local rain.

THE GENERAL STRIKE.

A wide response was made yesterday throughout the country to the call of those Unions which had been ordered by the T.U.C. to bring out their members. Railway workers stopped generally, though at Hull railway clerks are reported to have resumed duty, confining themselves to their ordinary work, and protested against the strike. Commercial road transport was only partially suspended. In London the tramways and the L.G.O.C. services were stopped. The printing industry is practically at a standstill, but lithographers have not been withdrawn, and compositors in London have not received instructions to strike. Large numbers of building operatives, other than those working on housing, came out.

The situation in the engineering trades was confused: men in some districts stopped while in others they continued at work. There was no interference with new construction in the shipbuilding yards, but in one or two districts some of the men engaged on repair work joined in the strike with the dockers.

Food:-Supplies of milk and fish brought into Kings Cross, Euston and Paddington were successfully distributed from the Hyde Park Depot and stations. The Milk & Food Contoller expects it will be possible to maintain a satisfactory supply of milk to hospitals, institutions, schools, hotels, restaurants and private consumers. Milk will be 8d. per gallon dearer wholesale and 2d. per quart retail today. Smithfield market has distributed 5,000 tons of meat since Monday.

Mails:- Efforts will be made to forward means of road transport the mails already shown as due to be dispatched very shortly from London. The position is uncertain and the facilities may have to be limited to mails for America, India & Africa.

At Bow Street Mr. Saklatvala, M.P., who was required as a result of his Hyde Park speech on Saturday to give his sureties to abstain from making violent and inflammatory speeches, was remanded for two days on bail.

Full tram and (or) bus services were running yesterday at Bristol, Lincoln, Southampton, Aldershot, Bournemouth, Chelmsford and Isle-of-Wight, and partial services in Edinburgh, Glasgow, Liverpool, Leeds, Northampton, Cardiff, Portsmouth, Dover, N.Derbyshire and Monmouthshire.

Evening papers appeared at Bristol, Southampton, several Lancashire towns and Edinburgh, and typescript issues at Manchester, Birmingham and Aberdeen.

The Atlantic Fleet did not sail on to summer cruise at at Portmouth yesterday. The men went on shore duty.

Road & Rail Transport:- There was no railway passenger transport in London yesterday except a few suburban trains. Every available form of private transport was used. A few independent omnibuses were running, but by the evening the railway companies, except the District and Tubes, had an improvised service. Among the railway services to-day will be:- 9.30 a.m. Manchester to Marylebone 9.30 a.m. Marylebone to Manchester; 10.10 a.m Marylebone to Newcastle; 9 a.m Norwich to London; 9 a.m King's Cross to York; 3 p.m. King's Cross to Peterborough; 9 p.m. Peterborough to King's Cross. L.M.S. Electric trains between Watford and Euston and Broad Street will maintain a 40 minutes service. On all sections of the Metropolitan Railway except Moorgate to Finsbury Park, a good service will run to-day from 5.40 a.m. The Underground hope to work a six minute service on the Central London Line to-day from 8 a.m. to 8 p.m. between Wood Lane and Liverpool Street. The following stations only will be open:- Shepherds Bush, Lancaster Gate, Oxford Circus, Tottenham Court Road, Bank, Liverpool Street. A flat fare of 3d will be charged.

The Prime Minister had an audience of the King yesterday morning.

There was no indication last night of any attempt to resume negotiations between the Prime Minister and the T.U.C.

The Government is printing an official newspaper, "The British Gazette" which will appear to-day, price 1d. It will be distributed throughout the London Area. Volunteers for the London Underground Railways and for L.G.O.C. omnibuses should communicate with the Commercial Manager's Dept. 55 Broadway, S.W.

The Prince of Wales returned to London from Biarritz last night travelling from Paris by air.

The British Gazette

Published by His Majesty's Stationery Office.

No. 2. LONDON, THURSDAY, MAY 6, 1926. ONE PENNY.

NATION CALM AND CONFIDENT

Gradual Recommencement of the Railway Services.

GOOD FUEL AND FOOD SUPPLIES.

Volunteers In Large Numbers At All The Centres.

OFFICIAL COMMUNIQUE.

A comprehensive survey of the situation on the second day of the General Strike shows the following salient features:-

An important part of the business of the country is held up, and increasing loss and inconvenience are falling upon all classes. Ample forces are available to maintain order.

The services of power and light are adequately maintained. The electric power stations have been manned, so far as it was necessary, with thoroughly efficient technical volunteers. The supplies of fuel and food are sufficient to maintain the life, though not the prosperity, of the country for many weeks to come.

METHODICAL DISTRIBUTION.

The distribution of milk and food is being methodically and regularly carried forward. The railway services are recommencing gradually and are already more numerous than on the second day of the railway strike in 1919.

Volunteers for national service of every kind are gathering at all the proper centres. Very large numbers of special constables have been sworn in, and more are being called for.

The nation remains calm and confident, and the people are bearing with fortitude and good temper the inevitable hardships of a national crisis.

TRAINS RUNNING.

Eleven Services on the Great Western.

[illegible]

HOW LONDON CAME TO WORK.

[illegible]

WHY WALK TO WORK?

CENTRAL LONDON	Six-minute service. Full service to-day.
METROPOLITAN	Services still improving.
PICCADILLY AND DISTRICT LINES	Volunteers standing by.
L.G.O.C.	200 'buses on the streets.
INDEPENDENT 'BUSES	Plentiful supply.

FOREIGN VIEWS OF THE STRIKE.

Liberty and the State.

THE WAY OF FASCISM.

[illegible]

Paris Press.

[illegible]

MIXED GERMAN FEELING

[illegible]

BELGIAN COMMENT.

[illegible]

STRIKERS AND PRESS.

[illegible]

RIFF PEACE PARLEYS.

[illegible]

"ORGANISED MENACE."

The Real Issue Behind the General Strike.

But Door Still Open.

[illegible]

TO CAR OWNERS.

Volunteers Required in the London Area.

[illegible]

THE PRINCE OF WALES.

[illegible]

T.U.C. FLOUTED

Hospital without Electricity.

WORK DISORGANISED

Operating Theatres Closed

[illegible]

YORKSHIRE INCIDENTS.

Bands of Pickets hold up Private Cars.

[illegible]

NOTICE TO PRINTING TRADE.

Official.

[illegible]

MOTOR-COACH HELD UP.

[illegible]

MESSAGE FROM THE PRIME MINISTER

Constitutional Government is being attacked. Let all good citizens whose livelihood and labour have thus been put in peril bear with fortitude and patience the hardships with which they have been so suddenly confronted. Stand behind the Government, who are doing their part, confident that you will co-operate in the measures they have undertaken to preserve the liberties and privileges of the people of these islands. The laws of England are the people's birthright. The laws are in your keeping. You have made Parliament their guardian. The General Strike is a challenge to Parliament and is the road to anarchy and ruin.

STANLEY BALDWIN.

CHANNEL SERVICES.

Shorter Routes Still Open

[illegible]

FOOD SUPPLY NORMAL.

[illegible]

PICKETS AND FOOD.

Men Fined For Disorderly Conduct.

[illegible]

ASHORE ON GOODWINS.

Ramsgate Tug Puts Out in Aid of Large Steamship.

[illegible]

FOR WOMEN AND GIRLS.

Mrs. Baldwin's Transport Organisation.

[illegible]

The Daily Mirror

NET SALE MUCH THE LARGEST OF ANY DAILY PICTURE NEWSPAPER

FRIDAY MAY 7 1926 PRICE ONE PENNY

FIRST PICTURES OF THE GREAT STRIKE IN LONDON

SCENE ON THE EMBANKMENT; THE ENDLESS STREAM OF TRAFFIC

TRAIN ARRIVING AT PADDINGTON YESTERDAY MORNING

DAILY EXPRESS

No. 8122. FRIDAY, MAY 7, 1926. ONE PENNY.

Train Services Improve.

FEWER DELAYS FOR WORKERS.

Many more trains were running yesterday in the London district and also in a number of the provincial centres.

It was a comparatively easy business on some of the London suburban lines for people to get to and from work. This, coupled with the fact that the immense road traffic was far better controlled, prevented the delays which most people experienced in reaching their offices on the first two days.

The following are the reports from the companies:—

G.W.R.—Trains between London, Ealing, Slough, Reading, Oxford and Worcester. Milk traffic handled satisfactorily.

Southern.—More than 330 trains in operation. Main line services to Bognor, Dover, Brighton, Portsmouth, Ramsgate, Hastings and Reading. Services steadily improving. Every important main line station has some service to London. Electric trains in London district at regular intervals.

L.N.E.R.— Considerable improvement in all suburban traffic. Service in each direction on all main lines and important branches. Expresses running between York and Newcastle and Duncaster and London.

L.M.S.—All milk taken from stations for delivery without a hitch. Skeleton suburban service in operation.

Metropolitan.—Fifteen minutes service each way between Baker-street and Harrow. Hourly trains between Baker-street, Rickmansworth and Uxbridge. Regular services on Northern route of the Inner Circle.

Omnibus Set on Fire.

Rowdyism broke out in the vicinity of the Elephant and Castle yesterday morning. A large crowd of "Roughs" gathered and one section of them stopped an omnibus which was going along St. George's-road.

They ordered the passengers, driver and conductor out of the vehicle and then set the omnibus on fire. It blazed furiously for some time but the fire was eventually put out by the fire brigade.

A large detachment of mounted police was later rushed to the district and complete order was restored.

Steelworkers' Return.

Over ninety per cent. of the men employed at the large steel works of Messrs. Whiteheads at Newport, Mon., returned to work yesterday, and both hot and cold mills are running normally.

Taxi Cab Strike.

London taxicab drivers have decided to join the strike. The decision was taken at a meeting on Wednesday night but there were many taxicabs on the streets yesterday.

THE INEVITABLE END.

By now the majority of the strikers recognise that failure is upon them.

Mr. Bromley, the Labour leader, has admitted in the House of Commons that they cannot prevail against the full resources of the Government. Those resources will be fully employed.

The Trade Union Congress with perfect truth define the issue as *for or against the strike.*

The vast majority of the nation including most of the strikers are against it. The British public are on the side of Parliamentary Government.

Only Trade Union discipline has saved the strike from total collapse. Its early breakdown is inevitable.

Buckrose By-Election.

The result of the by-election in the Buckrose Division of Yorkshire (following the retirement of Vice-Admiral Sir Guy Gaunt) was as follows:—

Major A. N. Braithwaite (C.)	12,089
Sir Harry Verney (L.)	10,537
Mr. H. C. Laycock (Soc.)	2,191
Conservative majority	1,552

The General Election result was:—Sir Guy Gaunt (C.) 13,966; Mr. H. A. Briggs (L.) 10,962. Conservative majority 3,004.

Bank Rate Unchanged

There was no change in the Bank Rate yesterday.

London Theatres.

Most of the London theatres are "carrying on."

Premier's Message

The following message from the Prime Minister was included in the second number of the "British Gazette."

"Constitutional Government is being attacked. Let all good citizens whose livelihood and labour have thus been put in peril bear with fortitude and patience the hardships with which they have been so suddenly confronted. Stand behind the Government, who are doing their part, confident that you will co-operate in the measures they have undertaken to preserve the liberties and privileges of the people of these islands. The laws of England are the people's birthright. The laws are in your keeping. You have made Parliament their guardian. The general strike is a challenge to Parliament and is the road to anarchy and ruin. . . . .

Stanley Baldwin."

Strikers Return to Work.

Numbers of strikers returned to work in various parts of the country yesterday and it is anticipated that their example will be followed by others to-day.

Transport workers at Grimsby reported themselves for duty yesterday morning. The tramcar services in the town are now the only section of road transport affected by the strike.

Seventy per cent. of the Liverpool tramwaymen returned to duty and services ran normally during the day.

Dock-keepers at Liverpool also reported for work and the electricians employed at Liverpool's main power house resumed their duties.

The number of strikers returning at the Wolverton carriage works of the London, Midland & Scottish Railway is increasing and 150 men are now at work.

Clerks and carpenters are working at McCorquodale's Printing Works, Wolverton.

Fulham Palace.

Fulham Palace has been offered by the Bishop of London as a neutral meeting place for future negotiations to end the trouble in the coal industry.

The Bishop announced that he had made that offer in a letter to Mr. J. H. Thomas, M.P., at a public meeting of intercession held in the Queens Hall.

"The raising of the standard of living of the poorest" said the Bishop, "is a worthy object, but past experience has shown that it is not to be attained by any short cuts."

The Bishop of London confessed that he had been made to feel a certain amount of bitterness towards those responsible for calling the strike, by the spectacle of little work girls having to walk six or seven miles to and from their places of employment.

Cricket.

Surrey v Glamorgan (Oval).
Glamorgan 264 all out
Surrey 196 for 4
(Shepherd out 117)

Essex v Australians (Leyton)
Australians 532 for 8
(Macartney 148 out, Woodfall 201 out)

Lancashire v Worcestershire (Manchester)
Worcestershire 194
Lancashire 282 for 7
E. Tyldesley 87 out

Cambridge v Yorkshire (Cambridge)
Yorkshire 176 & 185 for 9
Cambridge 176 all out

Saklatvala Goes to Prison.

TWO MONTHS' SENTENCE

Mr. Saklatvala, the Parsee Communist M.P. for Battersea chose to go to prison for two months at Bow-street Police-court yesterday rather than find two sureties for his good behaviour.

He was brought before Sir Chartres Biron, the chief Metropolitan magistrate, on remand, to show cause why he should not enter into recognisances and find sureties to be of good behaviour and keep the peace. The proceedings arose out of an alleged seditious speech, which it was stated Mr. Saklatvala had given at the May Day Labour demonstration in Hyde Park.

Police were on duty outside the Court-house and no crowd was permitted to collect. The public part of the court was filled with interested listeners. Among them was the wife of the defendant.

An order was made by the Magistrate that Mr. Saklatvala should find two sureties or as an alternative go to prison for two months.

"It is absolutely impossible for me to comply with that decision and to find the two sureties," declared Mr. Saklatvala.

Sir Chartres Biron: "Very well, you must go to prison for two months. No reasonable man can doubt but that the speech you delivered was seditious. Coming at this moment of particular difficulty, it was an act of criminal folly."

Thereupon the Battersea M.P. was removed to the cells.

Electric Supply.

Walthamstow Municipal electricity undertaking are discontinuing their supply to all trades except those connected with the food supply—including breweries.

Postponements.

Among the functions which have been postponed are the following: The Salvation Army Festival which was to have been presided over by Sir Thomas Inskip, the Solicitor-General, on Saturday, May 8th, at the Central Hall, Westminster; the British Ladies' Golf Championship arranged to be played at Harlech next week; the Annual Conference of the Licensed Victuallers' Defence League at Scarborough. The City of London School announce that they will open on Monday next. The National Road Walking Championship which was to have been held at St. Albans on Saturday next has been postponed.

Printed for and Published by The London Daily Express, Winters Printers, London, S.W.1.

126 Newspapers in the strike. The *Times* and the *Daily Express* are reduced here to single pages. The *British Gazette*, edited by Winston Churchill, and the trade union *British Worker*, were the 'official' strike papers.

127 (*left*) Inside the Labour Exchange at Snow Hill, Manchester.

128 and 129 Part of a mass demonstration in Hyde Park, October, 1932. (*above*) The police charging marchers near Marble Arch. (*left*) The demonstration was directed primarily against the hated Means Test.

130 (*above*) The Jarrow Crusade on the march, to the sound of mouth organs. The unemployment rate in Jarrow was over 80%. When Walter Runciman, President of the Board of Trade, calmly said that no official help could be given and that 'Jarrow must work out its own salvation', indignation was general. The march to London took more than a month. It got tremendous publicity, but the Government remained unmoved.

131 Demonstrations to obtain publicity. Unemployed men chain themselves to the railings of Stepney Labour Exchange.

132 (*below*) A demonstration at Grosvenor House, where Sir John Anderson was attending the Allied Brewery Trades Dinner.

THE STABILISING FORCES

133 (*opposite*) The King riding in Rotten Row.

134 King George V with Queen Alexandra, The Dowager Empress Marie of Russia and Queen Mary.
   Regard for the idea of royalty is superficial in Britain, but emotional attachment to members of the royal family has often been great. King George V acted in crisis as a moderating force. His advice to Stanley Baldwin during the General Strike that it would be 'a grave mistake to provoke the strikers' by passing provocative Orders and Bills was typical.

135 Stanley Baldwin, the greatest political force in maintaining the *status quo*, addressing the Women's Unionist Organization in 1928. 'You Can Trust Me', his posters said, and his appearance made this obviously true.

136 The first woman Cabinet Minister, Margaret Bondfield, Minister of Labour in the 1929 Labour Government, with her Under Secretary Jack Lawson.

The fear that women, when they got the vote, might use it to support subversion for some frivolous reason, proved quite unjustified. In voting terms British women were deeply conservative. Margaret Bondfield, though a Labour supporter, was irreproachably conservative and commonplace in thought and behaviour.

138–140 With the face and manner of a musical comedy star Edward, Prince of Wales, delighted the young by his jauntiness and modernity. (*above*) Saluted by an old soldier as he leaves the paddock at Epsom. (*opposite*) On his tour of South Wales, November, 1936, while still King Edward VIII. 'Something must be done', he said, a phrase which alarmed his Tory Ministers. (*bottom, right*) With the former Mrs Simpson in France, after their wedding. The King's abdication in December, 1936, was the scandal of the decade.

141 and 142 The new King George VI, the new Queen Elizabeth. Nervous, uneasy, afflicted by a bad stammer, George VI yet had something of his father's tough serenity.

143   The wedding of the King, while Duke of York, in April, 1923.

144 Crowds in Oxford Street on Coronation Night. They seemed amused rather than dismayed by having had three Kings in one year.

145   The King and Queen, with Princess Elizabeth and Princess Margaret.

146 Detached and paternal like Baldwin, Neville Chamberlain was even more reassuringly self-confident. Both men were great preservers, opposed by nature to change. Neither was disposed to take German Fascism very seriously.

147 (*opposite*) The Returning Officer declaring the poll at Epping Town Hall, Essex in November 1935 which saw Winston Churchill returned as the Member of Parliament.

148–150   During the years between the wars Eton and Oxford, full of ritual and tradition, undoubtedly represented stabilising forces in society. (*below*) Etonians buy buttonholes at Windsor for the 4th of June. (*opposite, top*) A group of Oxford undergraduates returning for the new term, 1934. (*below*) An Oxford election.

151 A speaker addresses the Oxford Union, December, 1938. In the following term he was President. His name is E. R. G. (Edward) Heath.

ARTS NEW AND OLD

152   A very early Shakespeare radio broadcast in 1923, probably from Marconi House.

153 (*above*) The Savoy Hill days at the BBC, before the opening of Broadcasting House in 1932, were remembered with nostalgia a few years later. The 2LO 'Invisible Band' on the air, December, 1923.

154 (*right*) Neville Chamberlain caricatured as the Wicked Uncle, in Unity Theatre's political pantomime, *Babes in the Wood*.

155 (*right*) Ralph Lynn and Winifred Shotter in one of the immensely success-ful Aldwych farces.

156 (*below*) *Plant In The Sun*, one of the lively propaganda plays put on by the Communist-inspired Unity Theatre, with Paul Robeson in the leading part and (*right*) Alfie Bass.

157 and 158   C. B. Cochran was the most successful theatrical showman of his time. His productions of plays, musicals, and above all revues were marked, Noel Coward said, by 'impeccable visual taste'. (*above*) Cochran's *1930 Revue*, with sketches and lyrics by Beverley Nichols and choreography by Balanchine. (*opposite*) Bernard Shaw can be seen among the audience.

159 'The British film, which had muddled through the silent era without distinction or success . . . remained notoriously devoid of either inspiration or vitality until the end of the Thirties', one American critic wrote, making an exception only for the documentary movement headed by Paul Rotha, John Grierson and Alberto Cavalcanti. (*above*) A scene from one of the few British film successes, Korda's *The Private Life of Henry VIII*, with Charles Laughton.

160 (*right*) Filming the arrival of the Royal Scot at Euston for an early British talkie, *Footsteps In The Night*.

161 (*below*) An Underground set for *Alias Bulldog Drummond* (1935), with Jack Hulbert and Fay Wray.

162 *Narcisse,* with Ninette de Valois and Henrietta Maicherska.

163 *Le Train Bleu* being danced for the first time in England, in 1923. From left to right: Sokolova, Dolin ('on that night he danced like a man in ecstasy'), Nijinska and Woizikowsky.

164   Massine, Vera Petrova and Boris Lissarevitch in *Mercury* (1927), 'a series of *poses plastiques*'.

165 In July, 1936, surrealism arrived in Britain, rather late, in the form of an exhibition at the New Burlington Galleries. Herbert Read, Wolfgang Paalen, Roland Penrose and André Breton are looking at Magritte's 'On The Threshold of Liberty'.
166 (*right*) The Surrealist Phantom wandered through the rooms, Salvador Dali lectured in a diving suit, 20,000 people visited the exhibition.

167 (*above*) In 1924 Jacob Epstein was asked to make a sculpture which would incorporate the idea of Rima, heroine of W. H. Hudson's *Green Mansions*. The result was unveiled in May, 1925, by Stanley Baldwin, then Prime Minister. A shiver is said to have been seen running down Baldwin's spine at the unveiling. Other reactions were stronger. The monument was called obscene, a horror, a bad dream of Bolshevism in art. In November it was daubed with green paint. Cleaned, it was daubed again. A letter demanding the removal of this piece of 'artistic anarchy' was signed by Hilaire Belloc and Sir Arthur Conan Doyle, among more predictable signatories like Sir Frank Dicksee (President of the Royal Academy) and Alfred Munnings. Rima weathered the attacks. She stayed and stays still, little remarked, in Hyde Park Bird Sanctuary.

168   The statue of Earl Haig by A. F. Hardiman was criticised on literal grounds. Military and veterinary critics had a field day when they saw photographs of the original model. The unhappy sculptor altered it and altered it again, and after the ceremonious unveiling in November, 1937, when 4,000 Service and ex-Servicemen lined Whitehall, *The Times* reflected with relief that it was not so bad after all. What if the horse was not one that Haig would have ridden, what if the stance rendered it unridable by anybody? 'It should be remembered that a bronze horse is not a flesh and blood horse', the paper sagely said. Like Rima, the Haig statue is now taken for granted.

169 On 15 December 1928, *Box and Cox* was shown at the Baird Television Studios. It was the first time that more than one person had been shown at a time on the screen.

170 (*below*) In 1936 the BBC began a service at Alexandra Palace.

171 (*opposite*) Tatiana Riabouchinska of the de Basil Ballets Russes in *Spectre de la Rose*.

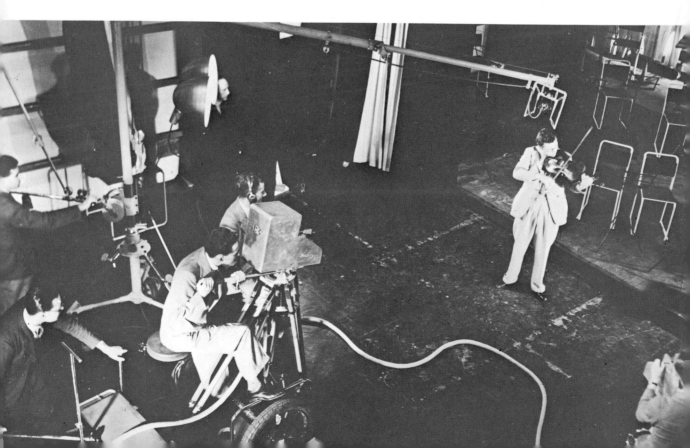

PREPARING FOR WAR

172 The Spanish Civil War was the great Left-wing cause of the Thirties. 2,000 volunteers joined the International Brigade. Nearly a quarter of them were killed, and another quarter were severely wounded. Some of the wounded arriving at Victoria Station, April 1938.

173 The deceits practised by the various Communist Parties involved in Spain, and their merciless persecution of other Left-wing groups, was little recognised at the time. This parade of the International Brigaders' Anti-Communist League took place in February, 1939.

174   Meeting at the Empress Hall after the return of the British members of the International Brigade, January 1939.

175 July, 1938. A demonstration in Trafalgar Square on the second anniversary of the beginning of the Spanish Civil War, to demand arms for Republican Spain. The official British policy of 'non-intervention' in effect favoured Franco.

176 There were persistent accusations that the police, in any fights between the Fascists and their opponents, took the Fascist side. Police clearing the way for a car carrying British Fascist officers through London's East End.

177 Many people thought that Hitler's attitude to the Jews would be softened when he gained power. The Jews themselves were not deceived. A protest march of 30,000 Jews in July, 1933.

178 One of the many meetings held in September, 1938, urging the Government to support the Czechoslovak stand against Germany.

37

179 (*left*) 'You would make the ideal Ambassador', Lord Londonderry told Joachim von Ribbentrop. 'You have the Führer's confidence, you know England, nobody likes the Bolshies, and we all want the facts straight'. Ribbentrop was German Ambassador in Britain from October, 1936 to March, 1938. 'Germany's Number One Parrot', as Goering called him, made himself unpopular by encouraging British appeasement of the Nazis.

180 (*right*) Ivan Mikhailovitch Maisky was Soviet Ambassador in Britain for 11 years, from October, 1932. He even survived the signing of the German-Soviet Non-Aggression Pact of August, 1939.

181 Chamberlain returns from Munich, waving the document which bought another few months of peace at the cost of the German occupation of Czechoslovakia.

Save my skin and damn my conscience.
And negotiation wins,
*   If you can call it winning,*
And here we are – just as before – safe in our skins;
*   Glory to God for Munich.*
And stocks go up and wrecks
*   Are salved and politicians' reputations*
Go up like Jack-on-the-Beanstalk; only the Czechs
*   Go down and without fighting.*

Louis MacNeice

182 (*left*) After Munich, preparations were made for the inevitable war.

184 (*above*) Trenches were dug in St James's Park, sandbags put round the pill-boxes at Buckingham Palace.

183 (*left*) Private air raid shelters were made like this one in Cardiff.

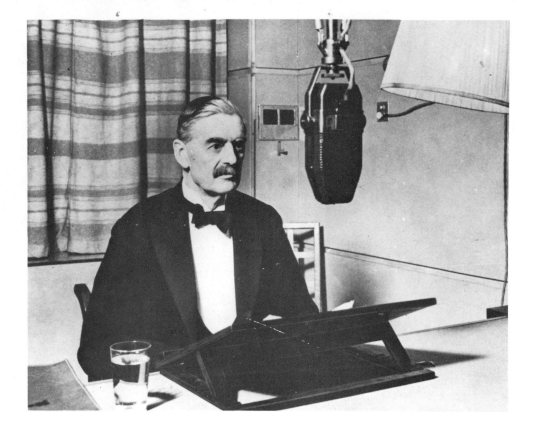

186 (*right*) June, 1939 Schoolchildren rehearse their evacuation from London, carrying belongings and gas masks.

185 (*above*) Chamberlain announcing the declaration of war on the radio, on the morning of September 3, 1939. It is a formal occasion. He is suitably dressed.

187   The news is read outside the Mansion House.
Ordered this year:
A billion tons of broken glass and rubble.

Roy Fuller

The clever hopes expire
Of a low dishonest decade:
Waves of anger and fear
Circulate over the bright
And darkened lands of the earth,
Obsessing our private lives;
The unmentionable odour of death
Offends the September night.

W. H. Auden